My Private French Class
Grammar and Conjugation
Level 1

Stéphanie Berton

First Edition

M'aidez Publishing

Stéphanie Berton – *My Private French Class, Level 1* | M'aidez Publishing

My Private French Class, Grammar and Conjugation, Level 1
Stéphanie Berton

M'aidez Publishing
http://www.maidezpublishing.com

Copyright © 2016 by Stéphanie Berton.

All rights reserved. Except as permitted under the United States Copyright Act of 1976, no part of this publication may be reproduced or distributed in any form or by any means, electronic or mechanical, including photocopying, recording, or stored in a database or retrieval system, without the prior written permission of the author.

ISBN 978-0-9888198-3-2

For this first edition, we would like to thank our team and all freelancers for their contributions to this great educational adventure!

Proofreading in English: Chris Zook
Correction en français et mise en page : Lucile Orliac
Couverture : S. Muñoz

Photo credits: © M'aidez logo, Dreamstime.com, Mime, © Andre Adams, book cover Eiffel Tower Isolated Photo, © Nerthuz, France Flag Background and Map Photo, © Cugianza84.

Books by Stéphanie Berton

The *My Private French Class* series is designed to work in conjunction with its companion textbook *My French Passport, Reading and Comprehension.*

My French Passport, Level 1, edition 1 (2013), ISBN-10: 0988819805

My French Passport, Les fêtes et traditions, Level 2, edition 1 (2014), ISBN-10: 0988819813

My French Word Search Puzzles, Les vacances, edition 1 (2015), ISBN-10: 0988819848

Introduction

My Private French Class s'adresse à **des adultes autodidactes** désireux de parler français couramment par le biais de supports se substituant à **une classe de F.L.E. (français langue étrangère) de niveau universitaire.**

Les niveaux débutants ont été établis de façon à construire des bases solides en grammaire et conjugaison, permettant ainsi de **maîtriser la construction d'une phrase**, phase cruciale de l'apprentissage d'une langue.

De la connaissance à l'automatisme

Notre méthode se fonde sur le principe simple d'une constante stimulation de la mémoire par de courtes mais fréquentes répétitions permettant au savoir temporaire de devenir permanent.
Au contraire de beaucoup de méthodes, l'élève est ici engagé à étudier, chaque mois, plusieurs points de grammaire et de conjugaison. La mise en pratique demeure hebdomadaire à travers de courts exercices. Même si le contenu du cours change mensuellement, la partie « Révisions » permet de maintenir en mémoire et d'approfondir les acquis des mois précédents. « Continuer d'apprendre sans rien oublier » sont les meilleurs mots pour définir cette méthode, qui permet d'acquérir les automatismes nécessaires à la maîtrise d'une langue.

Une participation active de l'apprenant

Cette méthode place l'étudiant au cœur même de l'apprentissage, qui s'accompagnera d'une recherche active du vocabulaire. En effet, nous avons délibérément choisi de ne pas traduire les mots nouveaux dont les contextes et significations multiples interfèrent dans les traductions. **L'usage du dictionnaire fait donc partie intégrante du cours,** ceci permettant également de renforcer la capacité de mémorisation.

Stéphanie Berton – *My Private French Class, Level 1* | M'aidez Publishing

Il est fortement recommandé de chercher les mots dérivés de même racine pour accroître rapidement et facilement la liste lexicale de l'apprenant. À titre d'exemple, une recherche du mot « chanteur » permet la découverte de son féminin « chanteuse », du nom commun « chanson », et du verbe « chanter ».
L'apprenant se doit d'être curieux !

À noter :
Nous voudrions attirer l'attention des élèves sur les choix et les sacrifices qui ont dû être faits pour faciliter l'apprentissage d'une langue pleine de règles, d'exceptions, mais aussi d'exceptions aux exceptions. De ce fait, nous avons parfois pris le parti de **simplifier une règle ou une traduction afin de la rendre plus assimilable au débutant en F.L.E.**
Ce livre devra donc toujours être utilisé tel un guide dont les règles et leçons ont été généralisées.

Ce livre respecte à la fois les typographies des langues française et anglaise. Le lecteur est ainsi exposé aux différences linguistiques dans ce domaine, et ce, pour une immersion complète dans la langue française.

Introduction

My Private French Class was conceived to provide college level **higher-education material to self-learners** aiming for fluency.

The beginning levels build strong foundations in grammar and conjugation, allowing students to master one of the most important language elements — **sentence structure**.

Turning knowledge into muscle memory

Our simple method constantly stimulates the memory with short but frequent repetitions to ensure temporary knowledge reaches the long-term memory, which is necessary for fluency. Unlike other teaching methods, ours engages the reader in the study of several grammar and conjugation lessons, which are reinforced each week through short exercises. As the class content evolves from month to month, the *Révisions* (Review) section helps keep memories active through constant recall, which strengthens the previously acquired knowledge.

"Keep learning, and never forget" is our method's goal. It is the key to enhancing the muscle memory that will help the student master the language.

An active learning method

We have deliberately chosen not to give a translated list of all vocabulary, since **using the dictionary is part of our active learning method, which powers memory retention and allows the reader to multiply the number of words learned**. Indeed, words may have multiple meanings or be used in a specific context.

We also strongly advise the reader **to look for words with the same root.** For instance, the dictionary search for *chanteur* (male singer) will lead the student to learn *chanteuse* (female singer), *chanson* (song), or *chanter* (to sing). Writing "*chanteur*, a male singer" in this book would take away the student's opportunity to learn more and go further. A good self-learner is a curious student!

Note

The student should be aware that some teaching choices and sacrifices must be made to facilitate the learning experience. Indeed, French is a language full of rules, exceptions, and (quite often) exceptions to exceptions. Therefore, we have decided, when necessary, to simplify a rule or a translation to make it more understandable and/or less overwhelming for a beginning student of French as a second language.

The reader should always keep in mind while using the book that it is to be used as **a guide, whose rules and lessons have been modified and/or simplified.**

Lastly, for full immersion in French culture, we have taken the trouble of respecting **the typographical rules for both French and English.**

Mode d'emploi

Cet ouvrage correspond à **douze séances d'exercices d'environ quatre-vingt-dix minutes de travail chacune**. Leur ordre chronologique devra être respecté du simple fait de **la difficulté progressive des exercices**.

La méthode conseillée est la suivante :

- Travail préparatoire
- Lire et comprendre les leçons.
- Mémoriser le contenu.
- Rechercher le vocabulaire de « C'est l'heure du dictionnaire ! »

- Séances 1, 2, 3 et 4
- Faire les exercices de la séance.
- **S'aider des leçons seulement pour la séance 1** afin de stimuler efficacement la mémoire. Veiller à respecter ce point crucial de notre méthode.
- Lire les réponses. Repérer et **comprendre ses erreurs**.

- Les jours suivants :
- **Refaire les exercices non réussis** de la séance en tentant de se rappeler ses erreurs.
- S'il y a toujours des incompréhensions, retravailler et mémoriser les réponses tout en veillant à intégrer les règles.

Il est conseillé de faire **une séance par semaine** seulement. Le laps de temps entre deux séances doit être consacré à **refaire continuellement les exercices jusqu'à complète réussite**.

À la fin de chaque séance, l'élève est invité à poursuivre son apprentissage en réinvestissant ses connaissances par **la lecture d'un texte de la série *My French Passport*. Le contenu grammatical et de conjugaison de cette série suit le programme de *My Private French Class*** pour permettre à l'apprenant de lire facilement et d'entrer dans une phase de prise de confiance. Au-delà de l'entraînement à **la compréhension écrite** et de **la découverte d'expressions idiomatiques** françaises, *My French Passport* constitue une fenêtre ouverte sur **la culture française** et offre également **des informations pratiques**.

Bon courage !

How to use this book

This book consists of **twelve, 90-minute exercise sessions**. The student should do them in the order given due to the **progression of the exercises' difficulty**.

The advised learning method is as follows:

* Preparatory work
- Read and understand the lessons.
- Memorize the content.
- Look up the vocabulary in the section called *C'est l'heure du dictionnaire !*

* Sessions 1, 2, 3, and 4
- Do the session's exercises. **Only use the lessons for Session 1**. The following sessions are dedicated to stimulating the student's memory. This is a crucial stage of our method, so keep it in mind.
- Read the answers in the back of the book to identify and **understand the mistakes made**.

* The following days:
- Do the same exercises while trying to remember and correct your mistakes.
- If pertinent, review and memorize the answer while increasing your understanding of the rules.

It is recommended to do only **one session a week** to allow the student the necessary time **to review and perfect the exercises**.

Each session will end with an invitation to **read a section of *My French Passport***, our reading and comprehension series, to continue the learning experience and reinforce the acquired knowledge. The grammar and conjugation **contents of both *My French Passport* and *My Private French Class* are intentionally identical** to facilitate the reading experience and increase self-confidence. More than just developing **reading comprehension** and exposing students to numerous **French idioms**, *My French Passport* presents **practical information about French culture**.

Bon courage !

Sommaire/Contents

Stéphanie Berton – *My Private French Class, Level 1* | M'aidez Publishing

I. Mois 1/Month 1

A. Leçons/Lessons

1. Saluer et se présenter/Greet and introduce yourself

Bonjour :	Good morning or good afternoon.
Bonsoir :	Good evening.
Salut :	Hello.

Bonne journée :	Have a nice day.
Bonne nuit :	Have a good night.
À demain :	See you tomorrow.
Au revoir :	Goodbye.
À bientôt :	See you soon.

S'il vous plaît : Please (to a few people or to be respectful).

S'il te plaît : Please (to one person you know well).

Merci : Thank you.

De rien : You're welcome.

Dialogue/Dialog

Julie : Bonjour, monsieur.
Good morning/afternoon, sir.

David : Bonjour, madame.
Good morning/afternoon, madam.

Quel est votre nom ?/Comment vous appelez-vous ?
What is your name?

Julie : Je m'appelle Julie, et vous ?
My name is Julie, and you?

David : Je m'appelle David. Enchanté. Comment allez-vous ?
My name is David. Nice to meet you. How are you?

Stéphanie Berton – *My Private French Class, Level 1* | M'aidez Publishing

Julie : Très bien, merci. Et vous ?
Very good, thank you, and you?

David : Bien aussi, merci. Voici mon cousin Paul.
I'm good too, thank you. This is my cousin Paul.

Paul, voici Julie.
Paul, this is Julie.

2. Le genre des mots/The gender of words

As you may already know, in French, words for objects have a gender. They are feminine or masculine. However, the gender of a noun is not always predictable, and logic does not always help. For example, *une chaise* (a chair) is feminine, whereas *un fauteuil* (an armchair) is masculine. In this case, both objects have the same use and structure, but they have different genders.

Memorize the gender when you learn a new noun and remember that the article will change accordingly in French. "The" will become *le* for a masculine word and *la* for a feminine word. "A" or "an" corresponds to *un* for masculine words and *une* for feminine words.

Here are a few tips that can be useful if you do not know the gender of a word. **Please keep in mind that these tips are very general and have exceptions.**

Nouns designating females are usually feminine, and nouns designating males are usually masculine:
une fille (a girl), un garçon (a boy), **une** mariée (a bride), un marié (a groom), **une** élève (a female student), un élève (a male student)

1)　**Masculine words are often:**
a)　The names of **languages**
le français (French), le chinois (Chinese)

b)　**Words** borrowed **from English**
le sandwich, le tramway, le T-shirt

Stéphanie Berton – *My Private French Class, Level 1* | M'aidez Publishing

Note

Words borrowed from Latin-based languages, like Spanish or Italian, already have a gender that is kept in French.
la salsa, la pizza, la paella, le guacamole…

c)   **Days, months, seasons, materials, colors, trees, weights and measures, compass points**
le lundi (Monday), le printemps (spring), le plastique (plastic), le rouge (red), le pommier (apple tree), le kilogramme (kilogram), le mètre (meter), le nord (north)

d)   **Words ending in -eau, -o, -isme**
le tableau (painting), le chapeau (hat), le stylo (pen), le vélo (bike), le socialisme (socialism)

2)   **Feminine words are often:**
a)   **Words ending in -ion, -té, -eur, -esse**
la nation, la population, la liberté (freedom), la quantité (quantity), la chaleur (heat), la princesse (princess)

b)   **Moral qualities, sciences, arts, fruits**
la gentillesse (kindness), la chimie (chemistry), la peinture (painting), la musique (music), la pomme (apple)…

Note

Did you notice that nationalities, languages, days, and months are not capitalized in French?

3. Les nombres de 0 à 69/Numbers from 0 to 69

0   zéro
1   un
2   deux
3   trois
4   quatre
5   cinq
6   six
7   sept
8   huit
9   neuf
10   dix
11   onze
12   douze
13   treize
14   quatorze
15   quinze
16   seize
17   dix-sept
18   dix-huit
19   dix-neuf
20   vingt
21   vingt **et** un
22   vingt-deux
23   vingt-trois
24   vingt-quatre
25   vingt-cinq
26   vingt-six
27   vingt-sept
28   vingt-huit
29   vingt-neuf
30   trente
31   trente **et** un
32   trente-deux...

40   quarante
41   quarante **et** un...

50   cinquante

51   cinquante **et un**...

60   soixante

61   soixante **et un**...

Les numéros de téléphone en France/Telephone numbers

05.49.23.06.15

Zéro cinq. Quarante-neuf. Vingt-trois. Zéro six. Quinze.

4. Des phrases simples/Simple sentences

C'est/It is, that is, this is
C'est + an adjective to express a feeling or a sensation

C'est chaud.	It's hot.
C'est froid.	It's cold.
C'est beau.	It's beautiful.
C'est laid.	It's ugly.
C'est gentil.	It's nice.
C'est difficile.	It's difficult.
C'est facile.	It's easy.
C'est loin.	It's far.
C'est près.	It's close.
C'est la vie !	That's life!
C'est dommage !	That's too bad!
C'est drôle !	That's funny!

Note

You say *c'est chaud* or *c'est froid* when you are touching something hot or cold. If you are discussing the weather, you say *il fait chaud* or *il fait froid*.

C'est + a singular word
C'est un chien. It's a dog.

Ce sont + a plural word or several singular words
Ce sont **des** chiens. These are dogs.
Ce sont monsieur et madame Martin. This is Mr. and Mrs. Martin.
Ce sont un chien et un chat. This is a dog and a cat.

Stéphanie Berton – *My Private French Class, Level 1* | M'aidez Publishing

Voici, voilà/Here is, here are
Voici is used with both singular and plural nouns. There is no conjugated verb.
Voici Marc. Here is Marc (when Marc is expected to arrive). This is Marc (while introducing somebody).
Voici un chien. Here is a dog.
Voici **des** chiens. Here are some dogs.

Il y a/There is or there are
Il y a is used with both singular or plural nouns, and as a question.
Il y a un chien. There is a dog.
Il y a **des** chiens. There are dogs.
Il y a **des** chiens ? Are there dogs?

5. Les nationalités/Nationalities

Generally, nationalities work just like regular adjectives: they agree in gender and number with the noun. In French, the nationalities are not capitalized, but the names of countries are.

	masculine adjective	feminine adjective	country/ continent
American	américain	américaine	les États-Unis (masc.)/ l'Amérique (fem.)
African	africain	africaine	l'Afrique (fem.)
English	anglais	anglaise	l'Angleterre (fem.)
French	français	française	la France
Spanish	espagnol	espagnole	l'Espagne (fem.)
Australian	australien	australienne	l'Australie (fem.)
Canadian	canadien	canadienne	le Canada
Italian	italien	italienne	l'Italie (fem.)
Belgian	belge	belge	la Belgique
Chinese	chinois	chinoise	la Chine
German	allemand	allemande	l'Allemagne (fem.)

Je suis **Cindy**. Je suis de Los Angeles. Je suis américaine.
Je suis Andrew. Je suis de Chicago. Je suis américain.
Cindy et Andrew sont américains.

Here you have two people, so *américain* takes the plural form with an -s. You may wonder, since Cindy is a female, why *américains* stays masculine. Well, in the French language, if you are referring to a group, and there is only one male or one masculine word, then the whole group agrees with the masculine gender.

Note

When a nationality is employed as a noun, you must capitalize it.

John est **un** Américain. John is an American.

6. Les pronoms sujets/Subject pronouns

One of the most basic things to learn when you study a language is the use of subject pronouns.

je	I
tu	you (one person with whom we can be familiar)
il	he, it (masculine)
elle	she, it (feminine)
on	one/we (familiar)
nous	we
vous	you (more than one person or to be respectful to one person)
ils	they (masculine or group with at least one masculine member)
elles	they (only feminine)

Voici Laurent. Il est français.
Voici un vélo. Il est petit.
Voici les garçons ! **Ils** sont gentils.
Voici les filles ! **Elles** sont gentilles.
Voici les filles et les garçons. **Ils** sont gentils.

Vélo is a "bike," and as an object, the pronoun "it" replaces the word in English. In French, *vélo* is a masculine word, so it is referred to as a "he," hence the use of *il* in the example.

Stéphanie Berton — *My Private French Class, Level 1* | M'aidez Publishing

Stéphanie Berton — *My Private French Class, Level 1* | M'aidez Publishing

C'EST L'HEURE DU DICTIONNAIRE !

Before you start working on the exercises, it is important that you take the time to look up the words we're going to use in a French-English dictionary. Committing a stock of key vocabulary words to memory is the first step in the learning process!

LES JOURS (masc. pl.)

lundi (masc.)

mardi (masc.)

mercredi (masc.)

jeudi (masc.)

vendredi (masc.)

samedi (masc.)

dimanche (masc.)

LES COULEURS (fem. pl.)

bleu (masc.)

jaune (masc.)

rouge (masc.)

noir (masc.)

blanc (masc.)

vert (masc.)

rose (masc.)

gris (masc.)

Note: These are the nouns.

LES FRUITS (masc. pl.)

poire (fem.)

pomme (fem.)

banane (fem.)

cerise (fem.)

olive (fem.)

 **Note**

Citron, abricot, kiwi and *ananas* are **masculine.**

LES QUALITÉS MORALES (fem. pl.)

gentillesse (fem.)

tendresse (fem.)

douceur (fem.)

bonté (fem.)

LES MOTS EN -isme

capitalisme (masc.)

socialisme (masc.)

cyclisme (masc.)

LES POINTS CARDINAUX (masc. pl.)

(masc.)

sud (masc.)

est (masc.)

ouest (masc.)

LES SAISONS (fem. pl.)

printemps (masc.)

été (masc.)

automne (masc.)

hiver (masc.)

LES MATÉRIAUX (masc. pl.)

plastique (masc.)

plomb (masc.)

granite (masc.)

cuivre (masc.)

LES ARBRES FRUITIERS (masc. pl.)

poirier (masc.)

pommier (masc.)

bananier (masc.)

citronnier (masc.)

cerisier (masc.)

olivier (masc.)

LES ARTS (masc. pl.) ET LES SCIENCES (fem. pl.)

musique (fem.)

peinture (fem.)

chimie (fem.)

astronomie (fem.)

biologie (fem.)

LES MOTS EN -eau

tableau (masc.)

chapeau (masc.)

cadeau (masc.)

château (masc.)

manteau (masc.)

Stéphanie Berton – *My Private French Class, Level 1* | M'aidez Publishing

B. Exercices/Exercises

1. Séance 1/Session 1

a. Saluer et se présenter
Compléter le texte./Fill out the blanks.

Julie : Bonjour, monsieur.

David : Bonjour, ________________. Quel est votre

________________ ?

Julie : Je m'________________ Julie, et vous ?

David : Je m'appelle David. ________________ (*Nice to meet you*).

Comment allez-vous ?

Julie : Très bien, ________________ (*thank you*). Et vous ?

David : Bien aussi, merci. ________________ (*This is*) mon cousin

Paul. Paul, ________________ (*here is*) Julie.

b. Les nombres/Numbers
Écrire les nombres en toutes lettres./Spell the numbers in French.

1 : ________________   6 : ________________

2 : ________________   7 : ________________

3 : ________________   8 : ________________

4 : ________________   9 : ________________

5 : ________________   10 : ________________

c. **Le genre des noms/Gender of nouns**
Choisir entre masculin et féminin et donner la règle./Indicate whether the word is masculine or feminine, and give the rule.

gender	word	rule
	liberté	
	française	
	pomme	
	nation	
	gentillesse	
	kilogramme	
	grec	
	t-shirt	
	bleu	
	tableau	
	allemand	
	jeudi	

d. **C'est + adjectif/It's + adjective**
Répondre selon le contexte/Answer according to the given context.
Ex.: You give hot rice to a child: c'est chaud.

1. You see a beautiful sky. →

2. You are eating a good dessert. →

3. You are touching ice. →

4. A child is giving you a flower. →

5. You think French is not easy. →

e. Il y a/There is or there are
Traduire en français/Translate into French.

1.   There is a girl.

2.   There is a girl and a boy.

3.   There are two kids.

f. Voici/Here is, here are
Traduire en français.

1.   Here are three boys.

2.   Here are two women.

3.   Here is my wife.

g. Les pronoms sujets/Subject pronouns
Traduire./Translate.

I →   we →

you (familiar, one person)   you (formal, one person, or a
    →   group) →

Stéphanie Berton — *My Private French Class, Level 1* | M'aidez Publishing

he →   they (masculine or group with both genders) →

she →   they (feminine) →

h. Les pronoms sujets : « tu » ou « vous »/Subject pronouns: *tu* or *vous*

Choisir entre « tu » et « vous »./Choose the correct answer: *tu* or *vous*.

1. Your father-in-law →

2. Your doctor →

3. Your best friend →

4. Your baker →

5. Your sister →

i. Les nationalités/Nationalities

Trouver la nationalité./Indicate the nationality.

1. Je suis de Chine, je suis _______________________.

2. Je suis de France, je suis _______________________.

3. Je suis du Canada, je suis _______________________.

4. Je suis d'Espagne, je suis _______________________.

5. Je suis d'Italie, je suis _______________________.

Reading suggestion: *My French Passport, Level 1*, Texte 1

2. Séance 2/Session 2

a. Saluer et se présenter
Trouver la bonne réponse./Select the right answer.

1.   You answer *quel est votre nom ?* with:

Voici Julie.
Très bien, merci.
Je m'appelle Julie.

2.   You answer *comment allez-vous ?* with:

Enchanté.
Très bien, merci.
Je m'appelle Julie.

3.   In the morning, you say:

Bonsoir.
Bonjour.
Au revoir.

4.   You say "bye":

Bonjour.
Au revoir.
À bientôt.

5.   You want to say "nice to meet you":

Enchanté.
J'habite ici.
Bien merci.

6.   You want to say "Here is my cousin":

Wayne est mon cousin.
Voici mon cousin.
Voici ma femme.

b. Les nombres
Écrire les nombres en toutes lettres.

1 : _______________   56 : _______________

20 : _______________   5 : _______________

2 : _______________   17 : _______________

11 : _______________   69 : _______________

30 : _______________   6 : _______________

3 : _______________   18 : _______________

12 : _______________   13 : _______________

41 : _______________   10 : _______________

4 : _______________

c. Le genre des noms
Choisir entre masculin et féminin et donner la règle.

gender	word	rule
	poire	
	poirier	
	printemps	
	manteaux	
	tendresse	

Stéphanie Berton — *My Private French Class, Level 1* | M'aidez Publishing

	pommier	
	lundi	
	mètre	
	nord	
	rouge	
	plomb	
	marketing	

d. C'est + adjectif
Traduire.

1. It's beautiful. →

2. It's hot. →

3. It's ugly. →

4. It's difficult. →

5. It's far. →

e. C'est, ce sont
Choisir entre « c'est » et « ce sont ».

1. Je suis Guy. _________________ Marc, mon ami.

2. _________________ des vacances formidables en Belgique.

3. Jean et Guy ? _________________ des cousins.

4. _________________ des fleurs.

5. _________________ une fleur.

f. Il y a
Traduire.

1.   There is a bird.

2.   There are two birds.

3.   There is a boy in the street (dans la rue).

4.   There are five girls in the street.

g. Voici
Traduire.

1.   Here is my friend Pierre.

2.   Here is a bird.

3.   Here is a girl.

h. Les pronoms sujets
Traduire.

I →   we →

you (familiar, one person)   you (formal, one person, or a
                                                  group) →
 →

he →   they (masculine or group with
                                                  both genders) →

she →   they (feminine) →

i. Les pronoms sujets : « tu » ou « vous »
« Tu » ou « vous » ?

1.   Your mother →

2.   Your husband/wife →

3.   Your brother →

4.   Your teacher →

5.   The letter carrier →

j. Les nationalités
Traduire.
Ex. Japanese : japonais/japonaise

	français masculin/féminin
African	
German	
American	

Stéphanie Berton — *My Private French Class, Level 1* | M'aidez Publishing

English	
Australian	
Belgian	
Canadian	
Chinese	
Spanish	
French	
Italian	
Portuguese	

Reading suggestion: *My French Passport, Level 1*, Texte 2

3. Séance 3/Session 3

a. Saluer et se présenter
Traduire.

1.   Goodbye.

2.   What is your name?

3.   How are you doing?

4.   Nice to meet you.

5.   My name is Julie.

6.   I am American.

7.   Here is my friend.

b. Les nombres
Écrire les nombres en toutes lettres.

11 : _________________   16 : _________________

12 : _________________   17 : _________________

13 : _________________   38 : _________________

14 : _________________   49 : _________________

15 : _________________   21 : _________________

   c. **Le genre des noms**
   Choisir entre masculin et féminin et donner la règle.

gender	word	rule
	week-end	
	citronnier	
	dimanche	
	vert	
	tentation	
	vélo	
	sud	
	cuivre	
	nord	
	générosité	
	casting	
	capitalisme	
	bonté	

   d. **C'est + adjectif**
   Traduire.

1.   It's close. →

2.   It's easy. →

3.   It's nice. →

4.   It's cold. →

5. It's beautiful. →

    e. C'est, ce sont
      Traduire.

1. It's a boy.

2. These are sandwiches.

3. It's a T-shirt.

4. These are lemons.

    f. Il y a
      Traduire.

1. There is a German woman.

2. There are two women.

3. There is one cat.

4.   There are nineteen flowers.

g. Voici
   Traduire.

1.   Here is my husband, Pierre.

2.   Here are Julie and Paul.

3.   Here is Sophie.

h. Les pronoms sujets
   Traduire.

you (to a group) →   they (feminine) →

you (to your friend) →   I →

he →   they (masculine or group with
                                  both genders) →

we →   she →

i. Les pronoms sujets : « tu » ou « vous »
   « Tu » ou « vous » ?

1.   Your sister →

Stéphanie Berton – My Private French Class, Level 1 | M'aidez Publishing

2. Your uncle →

3. Your cousin →

4. A police officer →

5. Your doctor →

j. Les nationalités
Trouver la nationalité.

1. Je suis de Belgique, je suis _________________.

2. Jean, tu es de France, tu es _________________.

3. Il est du Canada, il est _________________.

4. Elle est d'Espagne, elle est _________________.

5. Nous sommes d'Italie, nous sommes _________________.

Reading suggestion: *My French Passport, Level 1*, Texte 3

4. Séance 4/Session 4

a. Saluer et se présenter
Traduire.

1.   Julie: Good morning/afternoon, sir.

2.   David: Good morning/afternoon, ma'am. What is your name?

3.   Julie: My name is Julie, and you?

4.   David: My name is David. Nice to meet you. How are you?

5.   Julie: Very good, thank you, and you?

6.   David: I am good too, thank you. This is my cousin Paul. Paul, this is Julie.

b. Les nombres
Écrire les nombres en toutes lettres.

11 : _______________   66 : _______________

32 : _______________   57 : _______________

13 : _______________   8 : _______________

44 : _______________   19 : _______________

15 : _______________   20 : _______________

c. Le genre des noms
Choisir entre masculin et féminin et donner la règle.

gender	word	rule
	olivier	
	mardi	
	douceur	
	jaune	
	priorité	
	plastique	
	cyclisme	
	burger	
	cerise	
	château	
	pizza	
	pomme	

d. C'est + adjectif
Traduire.

1.   It's cold. →

Stéphanie Berton – *My Private French Class, Level 1* | M'aidez Publishing

2. It's hot. →

3. It's ugly. →

4. It's difficult. →

5. It's nice. →

      e. C'est, ce sont
      Compléter avec « c'est » ou « ce sont ».

1. Je suis Julie. _________________ Andrew, mon mari.

2. Je suis de San Diego. _________________ une ville en Californie.

3. Paul et David sont mes amis. _________________ des amis de France.

4. _________________ un chien.

5. _________________ deux chats et trois chiens.

      f. Il y a, voici, c'est, ce sont
      Traduire.

1. There is a dog.

2. There are dogs.

3.   Here is my friend, Julie.

4.   This is my wife, Sophie.

5.   These are sandwiches.

     g. Les pronoms sujets
       Traduire.

she →   they →

I →   he →

it (masculine word) →   we →

you →

     h. Les pronoms sujets : « tu » et « vous »
       Choisir entre « tu » et « vous ».

1.   A stranger →

2.   Two strangers →

3.   A receptionist →

4.   Your mother and your father →

5.   Your teacher and his wife →

i. Les nationalités

Trouver le bon pays./Indicate the right country.

1.   Je suis de _________________, je suis belge.

2.   Je suis de _________________, je suis français.

3.   Je suis du _________________, je suis canadien.

4.   Je suis d' _________________, je suis espagnole.

5.   Je suis d' _________________, je suis italien.

Reading suggestion: *My French Passport, Level 1*, Texte 4

II. Mois 2/Month 2

A. Leçons/Lessons

1. Les métiers/Jobs

It is easy to figure out the gender of a person referred to by his or her profession. Look at the ending!

masculine endings	feminine endings	translation
-er	**-ère**	
le boulanger	la boulangère	baker
le boucher	la bouchère	butcher
le cuisinier	la cuisinière	cook
-eur	**-euse**	
le chanteur	la chanteuse	singer
le serveur	la serveuse	server
-teur	**-trice**	
l'acteur	l'actrice	actor, actress
-ien	**-ienne**	
le pharmacien	la pharmacienne	druggist, pharmacist

Note

There is no need to place an article before a profession unless an adjective is present:

Jacques est boucher. Jacques is a butcher.

Jacques est **un gentil** boucher. Jacques is a nice butcher.

Stéphanie Berton — *My Private French Class, Level 1* | M'aidez Publishing

2. Les nombres de 70 à 99/Numbers from 70 to 99

70 (60 + 10)   soixante-dix
71 (60 + 11)   soixante **et** onze
72 (60 + 12)   soixante-douze
73 (60 + 13)   soixante-treize
74 (60 + 14)   soixante-quatorze
75 (60 + 15)   soixante-quinze
76 (60 + 16)   soixante-seize
77 (60 + 17)   soixante-dix-sept
78 (60 + 18)   soixante-dix-huit
79 (60 + 19)   soixante-dix-neuf

80 (4 x 20)   quatre-vingt**s**
81 (4 x 20 + 1)   quatre-vingt-un
82 (4 x 20 + 2)   quatre-vingt-deux
83 (4 x 20 + 3)   quatre-vingt-trois
84 (4 x 20 + 4)   quatre-vingt-quatre
85 (4 x 20 + 5)   quatre-vingt-cinq
86 (4 x 20 + 6)   quatre-vingt-six
87 (4 x 20 + 7)   quatre-vingt-sept
88 (4 x 20 + 8)   quatre-vingt-huit
89 (4 x 20 + 9)   quatre-vingt-neuf

90 (4 x 20 + 10)   quatre-vingt-dix
91 (4 x 20 + 11)   quatre-vingt-onze
92 (4 x 20 + 12)   quatre-vingt-douze
93 (4 x 20 + 13)   quatre-vingt-treize
94 (4 x 20 + 14)   quatre-vingt-quatorze
95 (4 x 20 + 15)   quatre-vingt-quinze
96 (4 x 20 + 16)   quatre-vingt-seize
97 (4 x 20 + 17)   quatre-vingt-dix-sept
98 (4 x 20 + 18)   quatre-vingt-dix-huit
99 (4 x 20 +19)   quatre-vingt-dix-neuf

3. Les articles/Articles

As we studied in the first chapter, French words are either feminine or masculine in gender and nouns are almost always preceded by an article in French. This article will be feminine or masculine depending on the noun that accompanies it. The list of French articles is long, and for now, we will start with the indefinite and definite articles. Each kind of article has a feminine, masculine, and plural form.

The indefinite article

un	une	des
masculine	feminine	plural

Il y a un chien dans la rue. There is a dog in the street.
Il y a **une** fille dans la rue. There is a girl in the street.
Il y a **des** chiens dans la rue. There are dogs in the street.

Note

Notice here that there is no plural article in English, whereas French has *des*.

Pronunciation

The French language is tricky because the final consonant of a word is usually not pronounced. However, you do pronounce this consonant in the word's feminine form when an -e is added.
Petit

Petite
You can hear the final *t* only in the feminine form: *petite.*

You also pronounce the final consonant of a masculine word if it is followed by a word that begins with a vowel, in which case you link the two words. This is called *une liaison.*
Un petit animal

In the same way, you can also hear the final consonant of plural forms. For instance, the final -s of the article *des* is silent in *des chiens*, but you can hear a [z] sound in *des oranges*.

The definite article

le	la	l'	les
masculine	feminine	masculine or feminine if the following word starts with a vowel sound	plural

Regarde le ciel ! Look at the sky!
Tu aimes la musique. You love music.

Voici l'oiseau ! Here is the bird.
Le chocolat est bon. The chocolate is good.
Voici **les** chiens de Marc. Here are Marc's dogs.

 **Note**

In this last example, using the plural, there is no article in English, but there is one in French.

Pronunciation tip (with *les*)

Remember to pronounce the *liaison* if *les* is followed by a word starting with a vowel sound!

J'aime les oiseaux. I love birds.

Sometimes there is no need to use an article

- If you use a number

Il y a **trois chiens**. There are three dogs.

- If you refer to a profession

Sophie est **danseuse**. Sophie is a dancer.

- After quantifying words like *"beaucoup de"*

Il y a **beaucoup de chiens** ici. There are many dogs here.

4. « Être » au présent de l'indicatif/"To be" in the present tense

je suis	I am
tu es	you are (informal)
il est	he is
elle est	she is
on est	one is/we are (familiar)
nous sommes	we are
vous êtes	you are (formal or to a group)
ils sont	they are
elles sont	they are (feminine)

5. Les couleurs/Colors

Find the meanings of these words in a dictionary.

masculine	feminine	translation
blanc	blanche	
gris	grise	
bleu	bleue	
vert	verte	
noir	noire	
rouge	rouge	
jaune	jaune	
rose	rose	
orange	orange	
marron	marron	

In French, adjectives usually appear after the noun they modify. We will see exceptions later, but for now, just remember their general position in a sentence.

The adjective's form varies according to the gender of the noun it modifies. Therefore, if the noun is feminine, you must write the feminine form of the adjective.
Voici une fleur blanche. Here is a white flower.

The adjective's form can also vary according to number. If the noun is plural, you must use the plural form of the adjective.
Voici des fleurs blanches. Here are white flowers.

 **Note**

There are exceptions! Adjectives that are also fruits (*marron* or *orange*) or flowers stay singular and masculine.
Il y a des oiseaux marron. There are brown birds.

Marron stays singular even if *oiseaux* is plural.

Il y a **des** chats orange. There are orange cats.

Note

Exceptions to exceptions exist too. *Rose* means pink, but it is also a flower (a rose), so *rose*, the adjective, should not agree in gender or number, but it does. It is one of the French language's "tricks" — an exception to the exceptions of the rule.

Il y a **des** fleurs roses. There are pink flowers.

The French language can be quite misleading, especially in regard to colors. In this book, we are intentionally keeping the rules simple for beginning, non-native speakers, but be aware that more nuances to the rules exist.

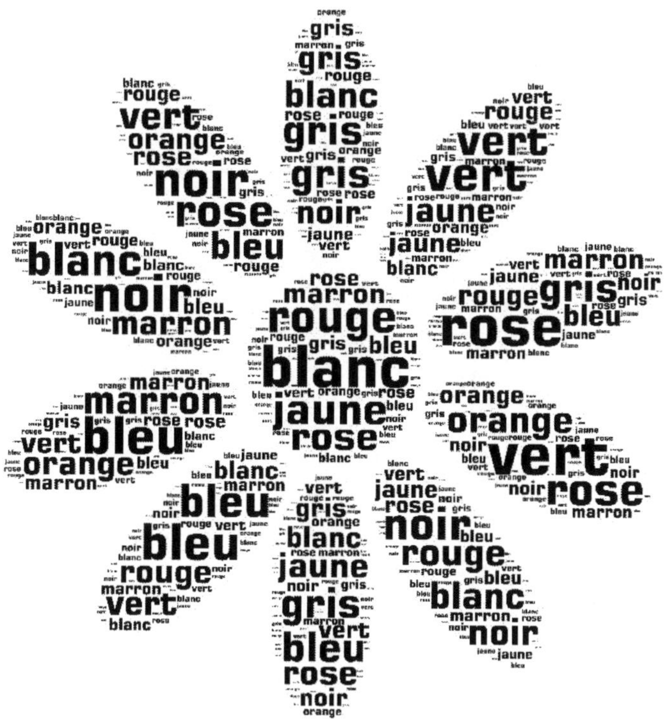

C'EST L'HEURE DU DICTIONNAIRE !

Before you start working on the exercises, it is important that you take time to look up the words we're going to use.

LES MÉTIERS (masc. pl.)

lecteur (masc.)/lectrice (fem.)

danseur (masc.)/danseuse (fem.)

rédacteur (masc.)/rédactrice (fem.)

dessinateur (masc.)/dessinatrice (fem.)

facteur (masc.)/factrice (fem.)

vendeur (masc.)/vendeuse (fem.)

instituteur (masc.)/institutrice (fem.)

mécanicien (masc.)/mécanicienne (fem.)

informaticien (masc.)/informaticienne (fem.)

comédien (masc.)/comédienne (fem.)

cuisinier (masc.)/cuisinière (fem.)

banquier (masc.)/banquière (fem.)

LES NOMS (masc. pl.)

papillon (masc.)

ciel (masc.)

langue (fem.)

nuit (fem.)

voiture (fem.)

soleil (masc.)

papier (masc.)

santé (fem.)

café (masc.)

soldat (masc.)

balle (fem.)

vanille (fem.)

beauté (fem.)

cadeau (masc.)

simplicité (fem.)

LES ADJECTIFS (masc. pl.)

malade

joli(e)

grand(e)

content(e)

mort(e)

fermé(e)

LES VERBES (masc. pl.)

regarder

aimer

jouer

B. Exercices/Exercises

1. Séance 1/Session 1

a. Les métiers
Choisir entre masculin et féminin et donner la règle.

gender	word	rule
	facteur	
	danseuse	
	lecteur	
	pharmacienne	
	rédacteur	
	mécanicien	
	acteur	
	informaticienne	
	actrice	
	cuisinier	
Révisions/Review		
	granite	
	bonté	
	vélo	
	pizza	

b. Les nombres
Écrire les nombres en toutes lettres.

70 : _______________   73 : _______________

80 : _______________   74 : _______________

90 : _______________   83 : _______________

71 : _______________   96 : _______________

72 : _______________   75 : _______________

c. Les articles

Choisir entre « un », « une » et « des ».

______ olivier

______ cerise

______ pizza

______ cerises

______ pomme

______ citronniers

______ vélo

Choisir entre « le », « la », « l' » et « les ».

______ ami

______ olivier

______ oliviers

______ cerise

______ vélos

______ rouge

d. « Être » au présent de l'indicatif

Conjuguer en utilisant la forme correcte du verbe « être »./Conjugate using the correct form of the verb *être*.

1. Je _______________ malade.

2.   Tu _________________ jolie.

3.   Il _________________ grand.

4.   Nous _________________ contents.

5.   Vous _________________ à Paris.

6.   Elles _________________ dehors.

e. **Les couleurs**
Compléter les phrases avec un adjectif de couleur. Attention au masculin, féminin et pluriel./Fill out the blanks with an adjective for a color. Pay attention to the masculine, feminine, and plural forms.

1.   J'aime les fleurs (red) _________________.

2.   J'aime les fleurs (white) _________________.

3.   J'aime les chapeaux (pink) _________________.

4.   Mes cousins sont malades. Ils sont (green) _________________.

5.   Le soleil est (yellow) _________________.

6.   La nuit est (black) _________________.

7.   Il y a une voiture (brown) _________________.

Révisions/Review

Traduire.

1.   My name is Julie. I am French. I am from San Diego.

2.   There are five dogs.

3.   It is hot!

4.   There is a pear tree.

5.   There are six pears.

6.   How are you?

7.   It's cold.

8.   Chinese is difficult.

9.   I am from Canada. I am Canadian.

10.   Here is my wife, Marie.

11.   There are fifty apples on (dans) the apple tree.

12.   Nice to meet you.

13.   We are happy.

Reading suggestion: *My French Passport, Level 1*, Texte 5

2. Séance 2/Session 2

a. Les métiers

Choisir entre masculin et féminin et donner la règle.

gender	word	rule
	factrice	
	danseuse	
	bouchère	
	pharmacienne	
	serveuse	
	mécanicien	
	vendeur	
	informaticienne	
	acteur	
Révisions		
	noir	
	papier	
	générosité	
	stylo	

b. Les nombres

Écrire les nombres en toutes lettres.

76 : _______________   97 : _______________

77 : _______________   88 : _______________

78 : _______________   81 : _______________

79 : _______________   90 : _______________

80 : _______________   91 : _______________

c. **Les articles**
Choisir entre « un », « une » et « des ».

______ sandwich

_____ poires

_____ manteau

_____ pommiers

_____ pomme

_____ télévision

Choisir entre « le », « la », « l' » et « les ».

_____ manteau

_____ lundis

_____ tendresse

_____ homme

_____ amis

d. **« Être » au présent de l'indicatif**
Conjuguer.

1. Elle ________________ fatiguée.

2. Nous ________________ tristes.

3. Je ________________ malade.

4. Ils ________________ occupés.

5. Vous _________________ stressés.

6. Il _________________ heureux.

7. Tu _________________ contente.

     e. **Les couleurs**
       Traduire.

1. I love red flowers.

2. I love blue cars.

3. I love the color black.

4. The sun is yellow.

Révisions

Traduire.

1. It's cold!

2. My name is David, and you?

3. She is from Africa. She is African.

4. Paul and Sophie, are you French?

5. Sixty cherries are red on the cherry tree.

6. There is a girl.

7. She is worried.

8. Nice to meet you.

9. What's your name?

Stéphanie Berton – *My Private French Class, Level 1* | M'aidez Publishing

10. I am Belgian.

Reading suggestion: *My French Passport, Level 1*, Texte 6

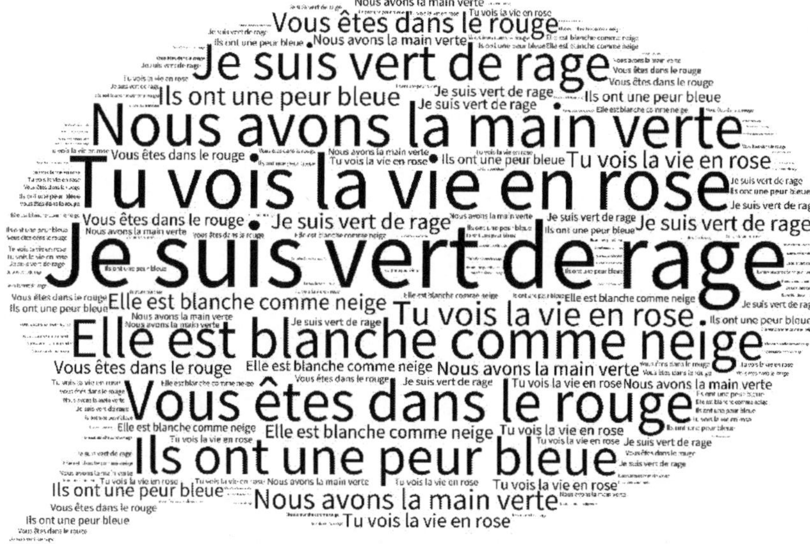

Stéphanie Berton — *My Private French Class, Level 1* | M'aidez Publishing

Séance 3/Session 3

a. **Les métiers**
   Choisir entre masculin et féminin et donner la règle.

gender	word	rule
	vendeur	
	institutrice	
	lecteur	
	comédienne	
	rédacteur	
	mécanicien	
	acteur	
	informaticien	
	travailleur	
Révisions		
	éducation	
	société	
	musique	
	pizza	

b. **Les nombres**
   Écrire les nombres en toutes lettres.

96 : _______________   85 : _______________

77 : _______________   92 : _______________

88 : _______________   82 : _______________

99 : _______________   94 : _______________

87 : _______________   70 : _______________

c. Les articles

Mettre au pluriel./Give the plural form.

Un ami →

Une chanteuse →

Le chocolat →

L'amie →

La fleur →

d. « Être » au présent de l'indicatif
    Traduire.

1. They are nice.

2. You are from Dijon.

3. I am Andrew.

4. She is happy.

5. We are tired.

e. Les couleurs
    Traduire.

1.   The black cat is sick.

2.   The red flowers are beautiful.

3.   I love yellow cakes.

4.   The sun is yellow.

Révisions

Traduire.

1. This is Mr. and Mrs. Martin.

2. The painting is beautiful.

3. Twenty-eight bananas are green.

4. There is one cat.

5. Here is David!

6. He is small.

7. There is a bike. It is white.

8. It is far.

9. Thank you.

10. We are Italian.

Reading suggestion: *My French Passport, Level 1*, Texte 7

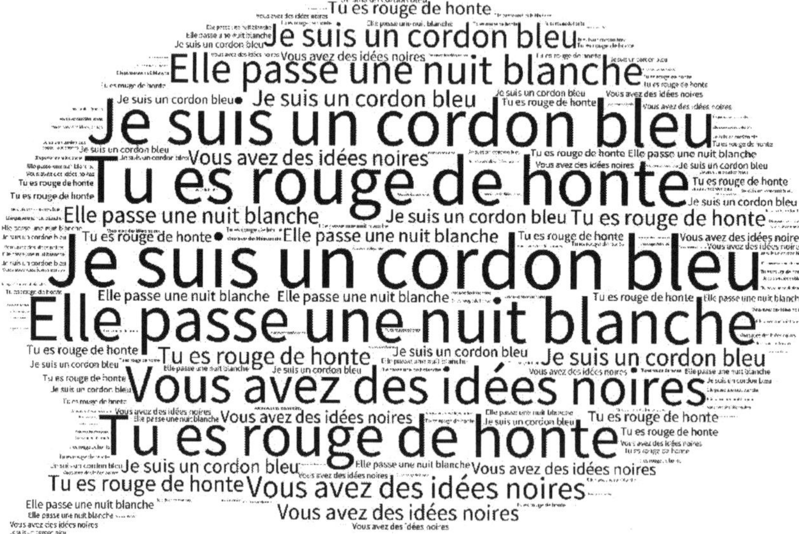

Stéphanie Berton — *My Private French Class, Level 1* | M'aidez Publishing

3. Séance 4/Session 4

a. Les métiers

Choisir entre masculin et féminin, et donner la règle.

gender	word	rule
	cuisinière	
	danseuse	
	banquier	
	comédien	
	chanteuse	
	mécanicien	
	acteur	
	informaticien	
	dessinateur	

<table><tr><td colspan="3" align="center">Révisions</td></tr></table>

gender	word	rule
	jaune	
	or	
	simplicité	
	cadeau	

b. Les nombres

Écrire les nombres en toutes lettres.

71 : _______________   76 : _______________

82 : _______________   75 : _______________

93 : _______________   86 : _______________

74 : _______________   97 : _______________

88 : _______________   73 : _______________

c. **Les articles**

Choisir entre « un », « une », « des » ou « le », « la », « l' », « les ».

1. _________________ socialisme est important en France.

2. Voici _________________ stylo.

3. Voici _________________ stylo de Pierre.

4. _________________ ciel est bleu.

5. _________________ école de Marie est fermée.

6. _________________ sandwich, s'il vous plaît !

d. **Les pronoms sujets**

Faire une phrase en français./Make a sentence in French with the correct forms of these words.

1. Je/être/fatigué(e)

2. Tu/être/malade

3. Elle/être/stressé(e)

4. Tu/être/préoccupé(e)

e. Les couleurs
Traduire.

1.   Sedona is a brown dog.

2.   Here is a white butterfly.

3.   I love red flowers.

4.   I love grey skies.

Révisions

Traduire.

1. We are from Italy; we are Italian.

2. My name is David. Nice to meet you.

3. Here are three boys.

4. She is American.

5. He is American.

6. Good night.

7. There are eight apples on the table.

8. She is German.

9. It is beautiful.

10. It is far.

Reading suggestion: *My French Passport, Level 1*, Texte 8

Stéphanie Berton — *My Private French Class, Level 1* | M'aidez Publishing

III. Mois 3/Month 3

A. Leçons/Lessons

1. La place des adjectifs/Placement of adjectives

In French, most adjectives are placed after the noun they modify.

Il y a un chat **gris**. There is a grey cat.

Of course, there are exceptions. Here is a simplified list of adjectives that precede the noun:

category	masculine	feminine	translation
beauty	joli	jolie	pretty
	beau bel + noun starting with a vowel sound ex. voici un bel homme.	belle	beautiful
age	jeune	jeune	young
	vieux vieil + noun starting with a vowel sound ex. voici un vieil homme.	vieille	old
	nouveau nouvel + noun starting with a vowel sound ex. Marc est un nouvel ami.	nouvelle	new
goodness	bon	bonne	good
	mauvais	mauvaise	bad
size	petit	petite	short
	grand	grande	tall
	gros	grosse	big

A good mnemonic device to remember these is the acronym BAGS, built from the first letter of each adjective category: **b**eauty, **a**ge, **g**oodness, **s**ize.

Stéphanie Berton — *My Private French Class, Level 1* | M'aidez Publishing

Il y a un petit chat gris. There is a little grey cat.
Voici **une** jolie fille. Here is a pretty girl.
Voici **une** vieille femme. Here is an old woman.

Exceptions to exceptions:
Ancien and *ancienne* (old/ancient/antique) frequently go after the noun.
C'est **une** voiture **ancienne**. This is an old/classic car.
C'est **une** vieille voiture. This is an old car.

When *ancien* means "former," it often goes before the noun.
Pierre est un **ancien** policier. Pierre is a former police officer.

Sometimes, you can switch the place of the adjective to change the meaning of the sentence. The adjective *sale* (dirty) is placed after the noun, as it is not part of the BAGS list.
Il a une tête sale. He has a dirty head.

But you can also find examples in which *sale* is before the noun.
Il a une sale tête. He looks tired/unhealthy/unfriendly.

For now, you do not need to worry about this. Just keep it in mind for later when you will be more familiar with the French language.

Stéphanie Berton — *My Private French Class, Level 1* | M'aidez Publishing

2. Être en train de, être sur le point de/To be in the process of, to be about to

Now that you know the conjugation of the verb *être*, you can make sentences to express actions in the present tense and the near future.

Near future	
Être sur le point de + infinitive	To be about to do something
Je suis sur le point de chanter. I am about to sing.	

Present tense	
Être en train de + infinitive	To be in the process of doing something
Je suis en train de manger un croissant. I am in the middle of eating a croissant.	

3. Mon, ton, son.../My, your, his...

My

Mon + a singular masculine noun: mon livre/my book

Mon + a singular feminine noun starting with a vowel or an *h*: mon amie/my (female) friend

Ma + other singular feminine noun: ma fleur/my flower

Mes + a plural (feminine or masculine) noun: mes livres/my books, mes fleurs/my flowers

Your (familiar)

Ton + a singular masculine noun: ton livre/your book

Ton + a singular feminine noun starting with a vowel or an *h*: ton amie/your (female) friend

Ta + other singular feminine noun: ta fleur/your flower

Tes + a plural (feminine or masculine) noun: tes livres/your books, tes fleurs/your flowers

His/Her

Son + a singular masculine noun: son livre/his or her book

Son + a singular feminine noun starting with a vowel or an *h*: son amie/his or her (female) friend

Sa + other singular feminine noun: sa fleur/his or her flower

Ses + a plural (feminine or masculine) noun: ses livres/his or her books, ses fleurs/his or her flowers

 **Note**

In English, "his" is used if the owner is a man, and "her" if the owner is a woman. In French, we do not refer to the owner's gender but to the gender of the object owned.

Ex. C'est **la** fleur de David. C'est **sa** fleur ! This is David's flower. This is his flower!

The owner is David, who is a man, but *fleur* is a feminine word, so the French language uses *sa*.

Ex. C'est le chien de David. C'est son chien ! This is David's dog. This is his dog!

Chien is a masculine word, so the possessive is *son* regardless of the dog's owner's gender.

Our
Notre + a singular (masculine or feminine) noun: notre livre/our book, notre fleur/our flower
Nos + a plural (feminine or masculine) noun: **nos** livres/our books, **nos** fleurs/our flowers

Your (formal/plural)
Votre + a singular (masculine or feminine) noun: votre livre/your book, votre fleur/your flower
Vos + a plural (feminine or masculine) noun: **vos** livres/your books, **vos** fleurs/your flowers

Their
Leur + a singular (masculine or feminine) noun: leur livre/their book, leur fleur/their flower
Leurs + a plural (feminine or masculine) noun: leurs livres/their books, leurs fleurs/their flowers

Stéphanie Berton – *My Private French Class, Level 1* | M'aidez Publishing

4. « Avoir » au présent de l'indicatif/"To have" in the present tense

j'ai tu as	I have you have (informal)
il a elle a on a	he has she has one has/we have (familiar)
nous avons vous avez ils ont elles ont	we have you have they have they have (only feminine)

Avoir is an irregular verb that means *to have,* but it is also used in situations that would not literally translate as "to have" in English. Languages often do not lend themselves to word-for-word translations, as in the examples below.

"To be" versus "to have"

In the following expressions, the English language uses *to be* where the French language uses *to have* to mean the same thing.

I am hungry (to be)	I am thirsty (to be)	I am ten (to be)
J'ai faim (to have)	J'ai soif (to have)	J'ai dix ans (to have)

I am hot	I am cold	I am wrong	I am right
J'ai chaud	J'ai froid	J'ai tort	J'ai raison

Stéphanie Berton — *My Private French Class, Level 1* | M'aidez Publishing

100 : cent
101 : cent un
102 : cent deux...

110 : cent dix
120 : cent vingt...

200 : deux cents
300 : trois cents
400 : quatre cents...

Note

When *cent* is followed by another number, *cent* does not vary in number (no final -s.)
210 : deux cent dix

1000 : mille
1002 : mille deux
1200 : mille deux cents
1306 : mille trois cent six

Mille stays singular.

2000 : deux mille (no -s)
3000 : trois mille (no -s)

LES VERBES (masc. pl.)

manger

regarder

danser

boire

acheter

chanter

parler

marcher

jouer

laver

tomber

cuisiner

dormir

LA FAMILLE (fem. sing.)

père (masc.)

mère (fem.)

sœur (fem.)

frère (masc.)

fils (masc.)

fille (fem.)

oncle (masc.)

tante (fem.)

Stéphanie Berton – *My Private French Class, Level 1* | M'aidez Publishing

grand-père (masc.)

grand-mère (fem.)

enfant (masc.)

LES ANIMAUX (masc. pl.)

souris (fem.)

chat (masc.)

chien (masc.)

serpent (masc.)

lapin (masc.)

papillon (masc.)

LES ADJECTIFS (masc. pl.)

intéressant(e)

préféré(e)

intelligent(e)

triste

gentil, gentille

mince

grand(e)

cassé(e)

DIVERS

œuf (masc.)

lait (masc.)

poupée (fem.)

bague (fem.)

gâteau (masc.)

chapeau (masc.)

ciel (masc.)

histoire (fem.)

voiture (fem.)

dent (fem.)

gant (masc.)

sol (masc.)

Stéphanie Berton — *My Private French Class, Level 1* | M'aidez Publishing

B. Exercices/Exercises

1. Séance 1/Session 1

a. La place de l'adjectif
Placer l'adjectif avant ou après le nom./Correctly place the adjective(s) before or after the noun.

1. Il y a un _________________ chat _________________

   (noir, petit).

2. Voici une _________________ femme _________________

   (belle).

3. J'ai un _________________ fils _________________

   (gentil).

4. David est un _________________ homme

   _________________ (intelligent).

5. Ralph est un _________________ chien

   _________________ (marron).

6. Ce sont des _________________ films

   _________________ (tristes).

b. Être en train de, être sur le point de
Traduire.

1. I am about to eat.

2. He is watching television.

3. We are about to dance.

4. They are about to drink cognac.

5. You are buying a car.

    c. Mon, ton, son...
       Traduire.

1. My sister →

2. My sisters →

3. My father →

4. My brothers →

5. Your mother →

6. Your sisters →

7. Your brother →

8. Your brothers →

9. His sister →

10. His brother →

11. Her sister →

12. Her brother →

13. His sisters →

14. Her brothers →

15. Its toy →

16. Our grandmother →

17. Our grandfather →

18. Our sisters →

19. Your uncle (to a group) →

20. Your uncles (to a group) →

21. Their daughter →

22. Their son →

23. Their children →

d. Avoir
Choisir la bonne conjugaison./Choose the right form
of the verb *avoir*.

1. Marie _________________ faim. (avons – ai – ont – a)

2. Marie et Pierre _________________ trois chiens. (ai – ont
– avez)

3. Mes enfants _________________ soif. (as – a – ont – ai)

4. J' _________________ raison et tu _________________ tort. (ont – a – as – ai) (ai – as – a)

5. Nous _________________ chaud, il fait 40 degrés dehors, en Californie. (avons – ont – avez)

e. **Les nombres**
Écrire les nombres en toutes lettres.

106 : _________________   6000 : _________________

220 : _________________   1407 : _________________

345 : _________________   2008 : _________________

400 : _________________   1709 : _________________

589 : _________________   1000 : _________________

Révisions

Traduire.

1. Brad Pitt is an actor. He is American.

2. I am happy.

3. I love red flowers.

4. I love coffee.

5. Spring is cold in France.

6. Marie is sick. We are worried.

7. There are 285 children.

8. My gift is beautiful.

9. The mechanic is nice.

Stéphanie Berton — *My Private French Class, Level 1* | M'aidez Publishing

10. I love yellow. It is my favorite color.

Reading suggestion: *My French Passport, Level 1*, Texte 9

Stéphanie Berton — *My Private French Class, Level 1* | M'aidez Publishing

2. Séance 2/Session 2

   a. La place des adjectifs
      Traduire.

1.   Here is an old woman!

2.   There are three big apples.

3.   There are ten beautiful flowers outside.

4.   France has an interesting history.

   b. Être en train de, être sur le point de
      Traduire.

1.   She is singing.

2.   I am about to eat.

3.   He is about to talk.

4.   They are walking.

5.   You (tu) are buying a car.

     c. Mon, ton, son...
       Traduire.

1.   My father →

2.   My mother →

3.   My sisters →

4.   Their dog →

5.   Their daughter →

6.   Their daughters →

7.   Our house →

8.   Our houses →

9.   Her father →

10.   Your hat (to one person, formal) →

11.   Your hats (to a group) →

12.   His sister →

13.   His bike →

14.   His bikes →

d. Avoir
Choisir la bonne conjugaison.

1. Nous ________________ raison : les chats mangent bien

les souris. (avons – ai – ont – a)

2. Elles ________________ besoin de gants. (ai – ont – avez)

3. Vous ________________ soif. (as – a – avez – ai)

4. Il ________________ vingt-huit ans et moi,

j' ________________ quarante ans. (ont – a – as), (ai – as – a)

5. Tu ________________ mal aux dents (toothache). (as – a

– avez)

e. Les nombres
Écrire les nombres en toutes lettres.

156 : ________________   6030 : ________________

229 : ________________   1407 : ________________

3450 : ________________   2008 : ________________

410 : ________________   1709 : ________________

689 : ________________   1000 : ________________

Révisions

Traduire.

1.   There is a butterfly.

2.   There is a yellow butterfly.

3.   There is a butterfly in the sky.

4.   He is from France.

5.   He is French.

6.   The black cat is sick.

7.   Paul is a butcher.

8.   Charles Trenet is a French singer.

9.   Édith Piaf is a French singer.

Reading suggestion: *My French Passport, Level 1*, Texte 1

3. **Séance 3/Session 3**

   a. **La place des adjectifs**
     Traduire.

1. There is a little cat.

2. This is beautiful music!

3. This is a good cake.

4. I love yellow flowers.

   b. **Être en train de, être sur le point de**
     Traduire.

1. He is eating.

2. We are about to play cards (**jouer aux cartes**).

3. You (**vous**) are cleaning the floor.

4. You are about to eat.

5.   They are walking.

    c. Mon, ton, son...
      Traduire.

1.   Your cousin is tall and skinny.

2.   My hat is brown.

3.   Their dogs are mean.

4.   Our daughter is about to sleep.

5.   Her bike is broken.

6.   My dogs are old.

    d. Avoir
      Traduire.

1.   I need my mother.

2.	You are right, and I am wrong.

3.	She has ten olive trees.

4.	They (feminine only) have three new dolls.

5.	We need two eggs.

e. **Les nombres**
Écrire les nombres en toutes lettres.

150 : _______________   6030 : _______________

229 : _______________   1427 : _______________

3450 : _______________   2018 : _______________

4010 : _______________   1809 : _______________

189 : _______________   3000 : _______________

Révisions

Traduire.

1. The apple tree is big.

2. David is a musician.

3. We are from England. We are English.

4. There are ninety men in the street.

5. It's beautiful.

6. It's hot.

7. It's ugly.

8. It's far.

9. It's a T-shirt.

10. Chinese is difficult.

Reading suggestion: *My French Passport, Level 1*, Texte 11

Stéphanie Berton — *My Private French Class, Level 1* | M'aidez Publishing

4. Séance 4/Session 4

    a. La place des adjectifs
    Traduire.

1.   Thomas is a smart child.

2.   Here is a brown dog.

3.   This is an old dog.

4.   This is a mean person.

5.   This is a small cake.

    b. Être en train de, être sur le point de
    Traduire.

1.   I am about to fall.

2.   They are dancing the tango.

3.   I am buying a ring.

4.   She is about to cook.

      c. Mon, ton, son...
         Traduire.

1.   Their cat is white.

2.   Our dogs are big.

3.   Your (familiar) hand is cold.

4.   My mother is tired.

5.   Your (formal) brother is tall.

6.   My brother is mean.

7.   Our rabbits are brown.

d. Avoir
Traduire.

1.   You are 12 years old; you need to sleep.

2.   I have two cars.

3.   She has a toothache.

4.   We need your car.

5.   They (masculine) have a friend.

e. Les nombres
Écrire les nombres en toutes lettres.

109 : ________________   1989 : ________________

999 : ________________   2000 : ________________

221 : ________________   2011 : ________________

678 : ________________

Révisions

Traduire.

1. She is sick.

2. They (feminine) are French.

3. I am from Dallas.

4. We are American.

5. You (familiar) are tall.

6. You (plural) are nice.

7. She is tired.

8. He is stressed out.

9. Here is a pen!

Stéphanie Berton — *My Private French Class, Level 1* | M'aidez Publishing

10.   There are seventy-one pink flowers.

11.   We have a dog.

12.   You have a nice cat.

13.   I have a beautiful hat.

14.   They are about to eat.

15.   Sophie and Paul, you are eating my cake!

Reading suggestion: *My French Passport, Level 1*, Texte 12

IV. Réponses/Answers

A. Mois 1

1. Séance 1

a. Saluer et se présenter

Julie : Bonjour, monsieur.

David : Bonjour, madame. Quel est votre nom ?

Julie : Je m'appelle Julie, et vous ?

David : Je m'appelle David. Enchanté. Comment allez-vous ?

Julie : Très bien, merci. Et vous ?

David : Bien aussi, merci. Voici mon cousin Paul.
Paul, voici Julie.

b. Les nombres

1 : un		6 : six
2 : deux		7 : sept
3 : trois		8 : huit
4 : quatre		9 : neuf
5 : cinq		10 : dix

c. Le genre des noms

gender	word	rule
fem.	liberté	ends in *–té*
fem.	française	a female French person (A man would be *français.*)
fem.	pomme	a fruit
fem.	nation	ends in *–ion*
fem.	gentillesse	ends in *–esse*
masc.	kilogramme	measurement

masc.	grec	the Greek language or a male Greek person (A female would be *une femme grecque.*)
masc.	t-shirt	word borrowed from English
masc.	bleu	color
masc.	tableau	ends in *–eau*
masc.	allemand	the German language or a German man (A female would be *une femme allemande.*)
masc.	jeudi	day of the week

d. C'est + adjectif

1. C'est beau !
2. C'est bon !
3. C'est froid !
4. C'est gentil !
5. C'est difficile !

e. Il y a

1. Il y a une fille.
2. Il y a une fille et un garçon.
3. Il y a **deux** enfants.

f. Voici

1. Voici **trois** garçons.
2. Voici **deux** femmes.
3. Voici ma femme.

g. Les pronoms sujets

je	nous
tu	vous
il	ils
elle	elles

h. Les pronoms sujets : « tu » ou « vous »

1. vous (at first)
2. vous
3. tu
4. vous
5. tu

i. Les nationalités

1. Je suis de Chine, je suis chinois/chinoise.
2. Je suis de France, je suis français/française.
3. Je suis du Canada, je suis canadien/canadienne.
4. Je suis d'Espagne, je suis espagnol/espagnole.
5. Je suis d'Italie, je suis italien/italienne.

2. Séance 2

a. Saluer et se présenter

1. Je m'appelle Julie.
2. Très bien, merci.
3. Bonjour.
4. Au revoir.
5. Enchanté.
6. Voici mon cousin.

b. Les nombres

1 : un	56 : cinquante-six
20 : vingt	5 : cinq
2 : deux	17 : dix-sept
11 : onze	69 : soixante-neuf
30 : trente	6 : six
3 : trois	18 : dix-huit
12 : douze	13 : treize

41 : quarante et un   10 : dix

4 : quatre

c. Le genre des noms

gender	word	rule
fem.	poire	fruit
masc.	poirier	fruit tree
masc.	printemps	season
masc.	manteau	ends in *–eau*
fem.	tendresse	ends in *–esse*
masc.	pommier	fruit tree
masc.	lundi	day
masc.	mètre	measurement
masc.	nord	direction
masc.	rouge	color
masc.	plomb	material, metal
masc.	marketing	word borrowed from English

d. C'est + adjectif

1. C'est beau.
2. C'est chaud.
3. C'est laid.
4. C'est difficile.
5. C'est loin.

e. C'est, ce sont

1. Je suis Guy. C'est Marc, mon ami.
2. Ce sont **des** vacance**s** formidable**s** en Belgique.

Stéphanie Berton — *My Private French Class, Level 1* | M'aidez Publishing

Note

Vacances is always plural.

3.   Jean et Guy ? Ce sont **des** cousin**s**.
4.   Ce sont de**s** fleur**s**.
5.   C'est une fleur.

f. Il y a

1.   Il y a un oiseau.
2.   Il y a **deux** oiseau**x**.
3.   Il y a un garçon dans la rue.
4.   Il y a **cinq** fille**s** dans la rue.

g. Voici

1.   Voici mon ami Pierre.
2.   Voici un oiseau.
3.   Voici une fille.

h. Les pronoms sujets

je   nous
tu   vous
il   ils
elle   elles

i. Les pronoms sujets : « tu » ou « vous »

1.   tu
2.   tu
3.   tu

4.   vous

5.   vous

j. Les nationalités

	français masculin/féminin
African	africain/africaine
German	allemand/allemande
American	américain/américaine
English	anglais/anglaise
Australian	australien/australienne
Belgian	belge/belge
Canadian	canadien/canadienne
Chinese	chinois/chinoise
Spanish	espagnol/espagnole
French	français/française
Italian	italien/italienne
Portuguese	portugais/portugaise

3. Séance 3

a. Saluer et se présenter

1.   Au revoir.
2.   Quel est votre nom ?
3.   Comment allez-vous ?
4.   Enchanté.
5.   Je m'appelle Julie/Mon nom est Julie.
6.   Je suis américain/américaine.
7.   Voici mon ami.

b. Les nombres

11 : onze
12 : douze
13 : treize
14 : quatorze
15 : quinze

16 : seize
17 : dix-sept
38 : trente-huit
49 : quarante-neuf
21 : vingt et un

c. Le genre des noms

gender	word	rule
masc.	week-end	word borrowed from English
masc.	citronnier	fruit tree
masc.	dimanche	day
masc.	vert	color
fem.	tentation	ends in *-ion*
masc.	vélo	ends in *-o*
masc.	sud	direction
masc.	cuivre	material, metal
masc.	nord	direction
fem.	générosité	ends in *-té,* moral quality
masc.	casting	word borrowed from English
masc.	capitalisme	ends in *-isme*
fem.	bonté	ends in *-té,* moral quality

d. C'est + adjectif

1. C'est près.
2. C'est facile.
3. C'est gentil.
4. C'est froid.
5. C'est beau.

e. C'est, ce sont

1. C'est un garçon.
2. Ce sont **des** sandwich**es**.
3. C'est un t-shirt.
4. Ce sont **des** citron**s**.

f. Il y a

1. Il y a **une** Allemande/Il y a **une** femme allemand**e**.
2. Il y a **deux** femme**s**.
3. Il y a un chat.
4. Il y a **dix-neuf** fleur**s**.

g. Voici

1. Voici mon mari Pierre.
2. Voici Julie et Paul.
3. Voici Sophie.

h. Les pronoms sujets

vous   elles
tu   je
il   ils
nous   elle

i. Les pronoms sujets : « tu » ou « vous »

1. tu
2. tu
3. tu
4. vous
5. vous

j. Les nationalités

1. Je suis de Belgique, je suis belge.
2. **Jean**, tu es de France, tu es français.

Note

Jean is the French name for "John," so it is masculine. *Jeanne* is the female name.

3.   Il est du Canada, il est canadien.
4.   Elle est d'Espagne, **elle** est espagnole.

Note

Espagnole takes the feminine form.

5.   Nous sommes d'Italie, **nous** sommes italien**s**.

Note

Italiens has an -s for the plural form.

4. Séance 4

a. Saluer et se présenter

1.   Julie : Bonjour, monsieur.
2.   David : Bonjour, madame. Quel est votre nom ?
3.   Julie : Mon nom est Julie/Je m'appelle Julie, et vous ?

4.   David : Mon nom est David/Je m'appelle David. Enchanté.
Comment allez-vous ?
5.   Julie : Très bien, merci, et vous ?
6.   David : Je vais bien aussi, merci. Voici mon cousin Paul.
Paul, voici Julie.

b. **Les nombres**

11 : onze	66 : soixante-six
32 : trente-deux	57 : cinquante-sept
13 : treize	8 : huit
44 : quarante-quatre	19 : dix-neuf
15 : quinze	20 : vingt

c. **Le genre des noms**

gender	word	rule
masc.	olivier	fruit tree
masc.	mardi	day
fem.	douceur	ends in *-eur*
masc.	jaune	color
fem.	priorité	ends in *-té*
masc.	plastique	material
masc.	cyclisme	ends in *-isme*
masc.	burger	word borrowed from English
fem.	cerise	fruit
masc.	château	ends in *-eau*
fem.	pizza	word borrowed from a Latin-related language in which *pizza* is feminine
fem.	pomme	fruit

d. **C'est + adjectif**

1.   C'est froid.
2.   C'est chaud.
3.   C'est laid.
4.   C'est difficile.
5.   C'est gentil.

e. C'est, ce sont

1.   Je suis Julie. C'est Andrew, mon mari.
2.   Je suis de San Diego. C'est une ville en Californie.
3.   Paul et David sont **mes** amis. Ce sont **des** amis de France.
4.   C'est un chien.
5.   Ce sont **deux** chats et **trois** chiens.

f. Il y a, voici, c'est, ce sont

1.   Il y a un chien.
2.   Il y a **des** chiens.
3.   Voici mon amie **Julie**.
4.   C'est **ma** femme Sophie.
5.   Ce sont **des** sandwiches.

g. Les pronoms sujets

elle   ils/elles
je   il
il   nous
tu or vous

h. Les pronoms sujets : « tu » et « vous »

1.   vous
2.   vous
3.   vous
4.   vous
5.   vous

i. Les nationalités

1.   Je suis de Belgique, je suis belge.
2.   Je suis de France, je suis français.
3.   Je suis du Canada, je suis canadien.

4. Je suis d'Espagne, je suis espagnol.
5. Je suis d'Italie, je suis italien.

B. Mois 2

1. Séance 1

a. Les métiers

gender	word	rule
masc.	facteur	job: un facteur, une factrice
fem.	danseuse	job: un danseur, une danseuse
masc.	lecteur	job: un lecteur, une lectrice
fem.	pharmacienne	job: un pharmacien, une pharmacienne
masc.	rédacteur	job: un rédacteur, une rédactrice
masc.	mécanicien	job: un mécanicien, une mécanicienne
masc.	acteur	job: un acteur, une actrice
fem.	informaticienne	job: un informaticien, une informaticienne
fem.	actrice	job: un acteur, une actrice
masc.	cuisinier	job: un cuisinier, une cuisinière
masc.	granite	material, stone
fem.	bonté	ends in *-té*, moral quality
masc.	vélo	ends in *-o*
fem.	pizza	word borrowed from a Latin-related language in which *pizza* is feminine

b. Les nombres

70 : soixante-dix

80 : quatre-vingts

90 : quatre-vingt-dix

71 : soixante et onze

72 : soixante-douze

73 : soixante-treize

74 : soixante-quatorze

83 : quatre-vingt-trois

96 : quatre-vingt-seize

75 : soixante-quinze

c. Les articles

un olivier
une cerise
une pizza
des cerises
une pomme
des citronniers
un vélo

l'ami
l'olivier
les oliviers
la cerise
les vélos
le rouge

Note

Put *l'* before a word starting with a vowel or a vowel sound.

d. « Être » au présent de l'indicatif

1.   Je suis malade.
2.   Tu es jolie.
3.   Il est grand.
4.   Nous sommes contents.
5.   Vous êtes à Paris.
6.   Elles sont dehors.

e. Les couleurs

1.   J'aime **les fleurs rouges.**

2.   J'aime **les fleurs blanches**.
3.   J'aime **les** chapeaux rose**s**.
4.   **Mes** cousins sont malade**s**. **Ils** sont vert**s**.
5.   Le soleil est jaune.
6.   **La** nuit est noire.
7.   Il y a une voiture marron.

Révisions

1.   Mon nom est **Julie**/Je m'appelle Julie. Je suis française. Je suis de San Diego.
2.   Il y a **cinq** chiens.
3.   C'est chaud !
4.   Il y a un poirier.
5.   Il y a **six** poires.
6.   Comment allez-vous ?
7.   C'est froid.
8.   Le chinois est difficile.
9.   Je suis du Canada. Je suis canadien.
10.   Voici ma femme Marie.
11.   Il y a **cinquante** pommes dans le pommier.
12.   Enchanté.
13.   **Nous** sommes content**s**.

2. Séance 2

a. Les métiers

gender	word	rule
fem.	factrice	job: un facteur, une factrice
fem.	danseuse	job: un danseur, une danseuse
fem.	bouchère	job: un boucher, une bouchère
fem.	pharmacienne	job: un pharmacien, une pharmacienne
fem.	serveuse	job: un serveur, une serveuse
masc.	mécanicien	job: un mécanicien, une

		mécanicienne
masc.	vendeur	job: un vendeur, une vendeuse
fem.	informaticienne	job: un informaticien, une informaticienne
masc.	acteur	job: un acteur, une actrice
masc.	noir	color
masc.	papier	material
fem.	générosité	ends in *-té*, moral quality
masc.	stylo	ends in *-o*

b. Les nombres

76 : soixante-seize

77 : soixante-dix-sept

78 : soixante-dix-huit

79 : soixante-dix-neuf

80 : quatre-vingts

97 : quatre-vingt-dix-sept

88 : quatre-vingt-huit

81 : quatre-vingt-un

90 : quatre-vingt-dix

91 : quatre-vingt-onze

c. Les articles

un sandwich
des poires
un manteau
des pommiers
une pomme
une télévision

le manteau
les lundis
la tendresse
l'homme
les amis

Note

Homme starts with a vowel sound.

d. « Être » au présent de l'indicatif

1. **Elle** est fatigué**e**.
2. **Nous** sommes triste**s**.
3. Je suis malade.
4. **Ils** sont occupés.
5. **Vous** êtes stressés.
6. Il est heureux.
7. Tu es contente.

e. Les couleurs

1. J'aime **les** fleurs rouge**s**.
2. J'aime **les** voitures bleue**s**.
3. J'aime **la** couleur noire/J'aime le noir.
4. Le soleil est jaune.

Révisions

1. C'est froid !
2. Mon nom est David/Je m'appelle David, et vous ?
3. Elle est d'Afrique, **elle** est africaine.
4. Paul et Sophie, vous êtes français ?
5. **Soixante** cerises sont rouge**s** dans le cerisier.
6. Il y a **une** fille.
7. **Elle** est préoccupée.
8. Enchanté.
9. Quel est votre nom ?/Comment vous appelez-vous ?
10. Je suis belge.

3. Séance 3

a. Les métiers

gender	word	rule
masc.	vendeur	job: un vendeur, une vendeuse

fem.	institutrice	job: un instituteur, une institutrice
masc.	lecteur	job: un lecteur, une lectrice
fem.	comédienne	job: un comédien, une comédienne
masc.	rédacteur	job: un rédacteur, une rédactrice
masc.	mécanicien	job: un mécanicien, une mécanicienne
masc.	acteur	job: un acteur, une actrice
masc.	informaticien	job: un informaticien, une informaticienne
masc.	travailleur	job: un travailleur, une travailleuse
fem.	éducation	ends in *-ion*
fem.	société	ends in *-té*
fem.	musique	art
fem.	pizza	word borrowed from a Latin-related language in which *pizza* is feminine

b. Les nombres

96 : quatre-vingt-seize
77 : soixante-dix-sept
88 : quatre-vingt-huit
99 : quatre-vingt-dix-neuf
87 : quatre-vingt-sept

85 : quatre-vingt-cinq
92 : quatre-vingt-douze
82 : quatre-vingt-deux
94 : quatre-vingt-quatorze
70 : soixante-dix

c. Les articles

Un ami → **des** amis

Une chanteuse → **des** chanteuses

Le chocolat → **les** chocolats

L'amie → **les** amies

La fleur → **les** fleurs

d. « Être » au présent de l'indicatif

1.   **Ils** sont gentils.

2. Tu es de Dijon/Vous êtes de Dijon.
3. Je suis Andrew.
4. **Elle** est heureuse.
5. **Nous** sommes fatigué**s**.

e. Les couleurs

1. Le chat noir est malade.
2. **Les** fleurs rouges sont **belles**.
3. J'aime les gâteau**x** jaune**s**.
4. Le soleil est jaune.

Révisions

1. Ce sont monsieur et madame Martin.
2. Le tableau est beau.
3. **Vingt-huit** bananes sont **vertes**.
4. Il y a un chat.
5. Voici David !
6. Il est petit.
7. Il y a un vélo. Il est blanc.
8. C'est loin.
9. Merci.
10. **Nous** sommes italien**s**.

4. Séance 4

a. Les métiers

gender	word	rule
fem.	cuisinière	job: un cuisinier, une cuisinière
fem.	danseuse	job: un danseur, une danseuse
masc.	banquier	job: un banquier, une banquière
masc.	comédien	job: un comédien, une comédienne
fem.	chanteuse	job: un chanteur, une chanteuse

masc.	mécanicien	job: un mécanicien, une mécanicienne
masc.	acteur	job: un acteur, une actrice
masc.	informaticien	job: un informaticien, une informaticienne
masc.	dessinateur	job: un dessinateur, une dessinatrice
masc.	jaune	color
masc.	or	material, metal
fem.	simplicité	ends in *-té*
masc.	cadeau	ends in *-eau*

b. Les nombres

71 : soixante et onze

82 : quatre-vingt-deux

93 : quatre-vingt-treize

74 : soixante-quatorze

88 : quatre-vingt-huit

76 : soixante-seize

75 : soixante-quinze

86 : quatre-vingt-six

97 : quatre-vingt-dix-sept

73 : soixante-treize

c. Les articles

1. Le socialisme est important en France.
2. Voici un stylo.
3. Voici le stylo de Pierre.
4. **Le** ciel est bleu.
5. **L'école** de Marie est fermé**e**.
6. Un sandwich, s'il vous plaît !

d. Les pronoms sujets

1. Je suis fatigué(e).
2. Tu es malade.
3. **Elle** est stressé**e**.
4. Tu es préoccupé(e).

e. Les couleurs

1. Sedona est un chien marron.

2. Voici un papillon blanc.
3. J'aime **les** fleur**s** rouge**s**.
4. J'aime **les** ciels gris.

Révisions

1. Nous sommes d'Italie ; **nous** sommes italien**s**.
2. Mon nom est David/Je m'appelle David. Enchanté.
3. Voici **trois** garçon**s**.
4. Elle est américaine.
5. Il est américain.
6. Bonne nuit.
7. Il y a huit pommes sur la table.
8. Elle est allemande.
9. C'est beau.
10. C'est loin.

C. Mois 3

1. Séance 1

a. La place de l'adjectif

1. Il y a un petit chat noir.
2. Voici **une belle** femme.
3. J'ai un gentil fils.
4. David est un homme intelligent.
5. Ralph est un chien marron.
6. Ce sont **des** film**s** triste**s**.

b. Être en train de, être sur le point de

1. Je suis sur le point de manger.
2. Il est en train de regarder la télévision.
3. Nous sommes sur le point de danser.
4. Ils sont sur le point de boire du cognac.

5.   Tu es en train d'acheter une voiture./Vous êtes en train d'acheter une voiture.

    c. Mon, ton, son…

1.   Ma sœur
2.   **Mes** sœurs
3.   Mon père
4.   **Mes** frères
5.   Ta/votre mère
6.   **Tes/vos** sœurs
7.   Ton/votre frère
8.   **Tes/vos** frères
9.   Sa sœur
10.   Son frère
11.   Sa sœur
12.   Son frère
13.   **Ses** sœurs
14.   **Ses** frères
15.   Son jouet
16.   Notre grand-mère
17.   Notre grand-père
18.   **Nos** sœurs
19.   Votre oncle
20.   **Vos** oncles
21.   Leur fille
22.   Leur fils
23.   **Leurs** enfants

    d. Avoir

1.   Marie a faim.
2.   Marie et Pierre ont **trois** chiens.
3.   **Mes** enfants ont soif.
4.   J'ai raison et tu as tort.
5.   Nous avons chaud, il fait 40 degrés dehors, en Californie.

e. Les nombres

106 : cent six
220 : deux cent vingt
345 : trois cent quarante-cinq
400 : quatre cents
589 : cinq cent quatre-vingt-neuf

6000 : six mille
1407 : mille quatre cent sept
2008 : deux mille huit
1709 : mille sept cent neuf
1000 : mille

Révisions

1. Brad Pitt est acteur. Il est américain.
2. Je suis content(e).
3. J'aime **les** fleurs rouges.
4. J'aime le café.
5. Le printemps est froid en France.
6. Marie est malade. **Nous** sommes préoccupés.
7. Il y a **deux cent quatre-vingt-cinq** enfants.
8. Mon cadeau est beau.
9. Le mécanicien est gentil.
10. J'aime le jaune. C'est **ma** couleur préférée.

2. Séance 2

a. La place des adjectifs

1. Voici **une vieille** femme !
2. Il y a **trois** grosses pommes.
3. Il y a **dix belles** fleurs dehors.
4. La France a **une** histoire intéressante.

b. Être en train de, être sur le point de

1. Elle est en train de chanter.
2. Je suis sur le point de manger.
3. Il est sur le point de parler.
4. Ils/Elles sont en train de marcher.
5. Tu es en train d'acheter une voiture.

c. Mon, ton, son...

1. Mon père
2. Ma mère
3. **Mes** sœurs
4. Leur chien
5. Leur fille
6. **Leurs** filles
7. Notre maison
8. **Nos** maisons
9. Son père
10. Votre chapeau
11. **Vos** chapeaux
12. Sa sœur
13. Son vélo
14. **Ses** vélos

d. Avoir

1. Nous avons raison : les chats mangent bien les souris.
2. Elles ont besoin de gants.
3. Vous avez soif.
4. Il a vingt-huit ans et moi, j'ai quarante ans.
5. Tu as mal **aux** (à + les) dents.

e. Les nombres

156 : cent cinquante-six

229 : deux cent vingt-neuf

3450 : trois mille quatre cent cinquante

410 : quatre cent dix

689 : six cent quatre-vingt-neuf

6030 : six mille trente

1407 : mille quatre cent sept

2008 : deux mille huit

1709 : mille sept cent neuf

1 000 : mille

Révisions

1. Il y a un papillon.
2. Il y a un papillon jaune.
3. Il y a un papillon dans le ciel.
4. Il est de France.
5. Il est français.
6. Le chat noir est malade.
7. Paul est boucher.
8. Charles Trenet est un chanteur français.
9. Édith Piaf est **une** chan**teuse** français**e**.

3. Séance 3

a. La place des adjectifs

1. Il y a un petit chat.
2. C'est **une belle** musique !
3. C'est un bon gâteau.
4. J'aime **les** fleur**s** jaune**s**.

b. Être en train de, être sur le point de

1. Il est en train de manger.
2. Nous sommes sur le point de jouer **aux** (à + les) cartes.
3. Vous êtes en train de laver le sol.
4. Vous êtes sur le point de manger./Tu es sur le point de manger.
5. Ils/Elles sont en train de marcher.

c. Mon, ton, son...

1. Votre/ton cousin est grand et mince.
2. Mon chapeau est marron.
3. **Leurs** chiens sont méchants.
4. Notre fille est sur le point de dormir.

5. Son vélo est cassé.
6. **Mes** chiens sont **vieux**.

d. Avoir

1. J'ai besoin de ma mère.
2. Tu as/vous avez raison et j'ai tort.
3. Elle a **dix** oliviers.
4. Elles ont **trois** nouvelles poupées.
5. Nous avons besoin de **deux** œufs.

e. Les nombres

150 : cent cinquante

229 : deux cent vingt-neuf

3450 : trois mille quatre cent cinquante

4010 : quatre mille dix

189 : cent quatre-vingt-neuf

6030 : six mille trente

1427 : mille quatre cent vingt-sept

2018 : deux mille dix-huit

1809 : mille huit cent neuf

3000 : trois mille

Révisions

1. Le pommier est gros.
2. David est musicien.
3. Nous sommes d'Angleterre. Nous sommes anglais.
4. Il y a **quatre-vingt-dix** hommes dans la rue.
5. C'est beau.
6. C'est chaud.
7. C'est laid.
8. C'est loin.
9. C'est un t-shirt.
10. Le chinois est difficile.

4. Séance 4

a. La place des adjectifs

1. Thomas est un enfant intelligent.
2. Voici un chien marron.
3. C'est un vieux chien.
4. C'est **une** personne méchante.
5. C'est un petit gâteau.

b. Être en train de, être sur le point de

1. Je suis sur le point de tomber.
2. Ils/Elles sont en train de danser le tango.
3. Je suis en train d'acheter une bague.
4. Elle est sur le point de cuisiner.

c. Mon, ton, son…

1. Leur chat est blanc.
2. **Nos** chiens sont gros.
3. **Ta** main est froide.
4. **Ma** mère est fatiguée.
5. Votre frère est grand.
6. Mon frère est méchant.
7. **Nos** lapins sont marron.

d. Avoir

1. Tu as **douze** ans, tu as besoin de dormir.
2. J'ai **deux** voitures.
3. Elle a mal **aux** (à + les) dents.
4. Nous avons besoin de ta/votre voiture.
5. Ils ont un ami.

e. **Les nombres**

109 : cent neuf
999 : neuf cent quatre-vingt-dix-neuf
221 : deux cent vingt et un
678 : six cent soixante-dix-huit
1989 : mille neuf cent quatre-vingt-neuf
2000 : deux mille
2011 : deux mille onze

Révisions

1. Elle est malade.
2. **Elles** sont français**es**.
3. Je suis de Dallas.
4. **Nous** sommes américain(e)**s**.
5. Tu es grand(e).
6. Vous êtes gentils (gentilles).
7. **Elle** est fatigué**e**.
8. Il est stressé.
9. Voici un stylo !
10. Il y a **soixante et onze** fleurs roses.
11. Nous avons un chien.
12. Vous avez un gentil chat./Tu as un gentil chat.
13. J'ai un beau chapeau.
14. Ils/Elles sont sur le point de manger.
15. Sophie et Paul, vous êtes en train de manger mon gâteau !

Made in the USA
San Bernardino, CA
18 April 2016